IAN BELL

ENGLAND CRICKETER

MR VIVEK KUMAR PANDEY

Made with ♥ on the Notion Press Platform
www.notionpress.com

Contents

Foreword

Short Biography Of Ian Bell & Life Style, Career etc. During Writing This Book No Character, No Religion & No Caste Are Harmed. It's Only For Study Purpose. We don't want to hurt anyone.

Preface

Author biography in English :

MY NAME IS VIVEK KUMAR PANDEY . I WAS BORN IN 30 SEP 2002,I AM FROM SURAT GUJARAT INDIA.MY DREAM WAS TO BE GOOD WRITERS ,MY FAMILY SUPPORTED ME TO SUCCESSFUL AND I CAN DO IT MY SELF.How do I write? That is a question, I believe, that can be honestly answered by me."CELEBRATING YOUNGEST WRITER AWARD WINNER IN GUJARAT 1ST RANK" MR PANDEY JI . I may think I did a good job writing something. The reader is the one who decides the quality of my writing. I do find writing to be natural to me and therefore find it to be a real challenge. My trick as a challenged writer is to do the best I can and know that I am happy with the final outcome. It may take a while to do my best and there may be quite a few problems I run into along the way.

I am not a greedy person those who are thinking about me and my self I never tried it anyone people suffering from sadness ,I trying to get promoted people suffering from happiness and joy in your Life Time. Now in current situation in India and also world people are unemployed and have no many but our indian governor help to people to get free food from ration card , i also take part in leadership team ,i am Motivational speaker , Film script writer. There was my two dream firstly writer and secondly actor & also my own film is upcoming soon i done almost completely completed script for my film .I AM GOING TO SAY WORD OF HEART TOUCH OUT PLEASE READ IT" , firstly i thanks my father he supports me in this field they always getting inspired me by own his words and behavior ,they always said that he was a biggest person in the world in future and also they purchase fruit and chocolate for me in anytime & anyway , firstly my father buy him then call me Vivek you want a chocolate i will say yes papa but how many tell me ,papa: you tell me how much i buy him i told 1 or 2 chocolate but my father purchase whole the boxes of chocolate and they get suprised me. MY FATHER WAS BORN IN " 20 SEPTEMBER" 1971 IN INDIA.

1) MY FATHER FAVORITE CLOTHES IS KURTA PAIJMA AND ALSO STYLES SHOE

2) FAVORITE SINGER IS KISHORE DA

3) FAVORITE STATE GUJARAT AND KOLKATA , HIS VILLAGE IN BIHAR

4) FAVORITE COLOR BLACK AND WHITE

THEY ALSO LOVE cricket like IPL and one day t-20 .they also like watching a News daily and heard the song daily ,they also interested in tik tok video but in current time tik tok is banned in india but also few videos are in you tube. In lockdown time my family and me very enjoy day daily. my father play daily ludo with his sister and son, daughter.they always loved tea and coffee anytime call me . I make it tea for my father but some reason after the April to june they are suffering from fever and cough , weakness on 6 June 2020 my father death. they not told me say bye bye his life. After death of 6 June on 10 june my mom and dad anniversary.but my father is Best in the world they can do anything for me please take care of father and respect it of your parents.

ONE

IAN BELL

- **Ian Bell**

1. Short Biography Of Ian Bell & Life Style, Career etc. During Writing This Book No Character, No Religion & No Caste Are Harmed. It's Only For Study Purpose. We don't want to hurt anyone.

Ian Bell (born 11 April 1982) is an English former cricketer who played international cricket in all formats for the England cricket team and county cricket for Warwickshire County Cricket Club. A right-handed higher/ middle order batsman, described in The Times as an "exquisite rapier," with a strong cover drive, Bell was also an occasional right-arm medium pace bowler and a slip fielder. He was also noted for his sharp reflexes and often fielded in close catching positions. He scored twenty-two Test centuries and four One Day International (ODI) 100s.

In the 2006 New Year Honours List, Bell was appointed Member of the Order of the British Empire for his role in the successful Ashes campaign of 2005. In November 2006, he was awarded the Emerging Player of the Year award by the International Cricket Council. During 2008 and 2009, he was a more infrequent member of the England teams – however he reclaimed his Test place during the 2009 Ashes, which England won, and featured in several ODIs the following year. During 2010, he captained Warwickshire to victory in the CB40 final before scoring his first Ashes century the following winter as he helped England retain the Ashes down-under. Warwickshire County Cricket Club awarded Bell a benefit in 2011.

In July 2012, Bell signed a new three-year contract with Warwickshire extending his stay at the club at least till 2015. In November 2015, England selectors announced that Bell would be dropped from the English side ahead of the test series with South Africa. In August 2016, it was announced that Bell would be playing for the Perth Scorchers in the 2016–17 Big Bash League season. In August 2018, Bell scored his 20,000th run in first-class cricket. In September 2020, Bell announced his retirement, revealing that his final game for Warwickshire would be a T20 match against Glamorgan.

- **Ian Bell Education and life**

Bell's family hailed from Dunchurch, near Rugby and he played for the local cricket club as a junior. Bell was educated at Princethorpe College, a Roman Catholic independent school in the nearby village of Princethorpe and made the 1st XI in year 7. He also attended Coventry City's football school of excellence, despite being a supporter of Aston Villa (those two football clubs are traditional rivals), and played for Coventry and North Warwickshire Cricket Club. His brother Keith, born two years later, has played amateur cricket for Staffordshire, and has also played seven games for the Warwickshire Second XI.

- **Ian Bell career**

Bell made three appearances for Warwickshire's second team in 1998, his next matches at senior level were with the England Under-19 cricket team on their tour of New Zealand that winter. He made 91 in the first innings of the first Test, and 115 in the first innings of the third; Dayle Hadlee called Bell "the best 16-year-old I've ever seen", and he was often compared with former England captain Mike Atherton. Bell played in several more Under-19 series, captaining the team at home against Sri Lanka in 2000, in their 2000/01 tour of India, and for the first match at home against West Indies in 2001.

By this time Bell had made his first-class debut, appearing in a single match for the Warwickshire first team in September 1999, but was out for a duck in his only innings and played no further part at that level until 2000/01, when he followed on from his Under-19 matches by playing for England A against the Leeward Islands in the Busta Cup tournament game in Anguilla.

Bell broke into the Warwickshire first-team in 2001 as he scored 836 runs in 16 innings including three centuries and two scores of 98. His first century, a score of 130 against Oxford UCCE, made him the county's youngest ever centurion at 19 years and 56 days. He also became the county's youngest capped player ever when Warwickshire awarded him a county cap on the final day of the season.Bell was named in the first intake of the ECB National Academy who spent the 2001/02 winter in

Australia. The day after he returned home from Adelaide he was brought into the full England Test squad to cover for the injured Mark Butcher on the New Zealand tour.

In 2002 Bell's four-day form fell away as he scored 658 at an average of 24.37 however he was instrumental in the county's Benson & Hedges Cup success. He top-scored in the Quarter-final (scoring 85 not out), Semi-final (46) and Final (65 not out), the latter performance winning him the Gold Award in the last ever Benson & Hedges Cup final.

Bell's best form in 2003 once again came in the one-day format, he scored 779 runs at 28.85 in the County Championship compared to 560 runs at 43.07 in the National League, his best performance came at Chelmsford where he scored his maiden one-day century, 125 off 113 deliveries, as well as taking 5/41, his best one-day bowling figures. This was only the second time a Warwickshire player had achieved this feat.

After two poor seasons Bell was back to his best in 2004, he scored 1498 Championship runs which included six centuries. One of the six was a career-best 262 not out against Sussex; the innings lasting ten minutes short of ten hours made him the county's youngest ever double-centurion. In late July he began an impressive sequence of four centuries in five first-class innings, the other being a score of 96 not out. The centuries in both innings against Lancashire were the first by a Warwickshire batsman against an authentic attack (David Hemp achieved the feat against declaration bowling) since Brian Lara in 1994. This run of form led to him being brought into the England Test squad when Graham Thorpe was left doubtful with a finger injury.

- **Ian Bell International career in 2004: West Indies**

Bell made his international debut in the final match of the Test series against the West Indies at The Oval. He hit 70, batting at number five in England's first innings; he was not required to bat again as England forced the West Indies to follow on and won the game by ten wickets.

- **Ian Bell in 2004/05: Zimbabwe and South Africa**

Bell was selected as part of the squad to tour Zimbabwe and South Africa and he made his One Day International debut alongside Kevin Pietersen against Zimbabwe at Harare. Bell opened the innings and hit 75, which earned him his first ODI man-of-the-match award. He played all four matches of the series averaging 40.75. Although he was not chosen for any of the Tests against South Africa, he was selected for the first four of seven ODI matches but struggled, making 26 runs in three innings.

- **Ian Bell in 2005: Bangladesh and The Ashes**

In 2005, Bell enjoyed a superb start to the season, scoring 480 first-class runs in April alone to break Graeme Hick's 17-year-old record. He was recalled to the England team for the two-Test series against Bangladesh, however England's innings victories in both Tests allowed him only two innings. In the first Test at Lord's, Bell made 65 not out, and in the second at Chester-le-Street he scored 162 not out, in the process becoming the first Englishman since Leslie Ames in 1935 to score over 100 runs before lunch in a Test match.

For the 2005 Ashes series, three players – Bell, Graham Thorpe and Kevin Pietersen – were in the running for two spots in the team, and Bell and Pietersen were preferred to

Thorpe. Before the first Test at Lord's, Bell's test average was 297, rising to 303 just before he was out, the sixth highest average at any point of a player's career of all time. Bell failed in the first two matches, at Lord's and Edgbaston, but in the third Test at Old Trafford he overcame early struggles against Shane Warne to post a half-century in each innings. However, he only scored six runs in four innings in the fourth and fifth Tests, including a pair at the Oval, leaving him with a batting average for the series of only 17.10, by far the lowest of the English batsmen. He was appointed Member of the Order of the British Empire in the 2006 New Year Honours. Despite England winning the Ashes back and being appointed , Bell has since described the 2005 Ashes as a low point during which he doubted himself.

- **Ian Bell in 2005/06: Pakistan and India**

Despite failing against Australia, he was included in the 17-man squad for the winter tour of Pakistan. There was speculation in the press that he would not be included in the Test team, but when Michael Vaughan was injured before the first Test, Bell got another opportunity. He took it, scoring a century and two half-centuries in the three-match series, and becoming England's top scorer in the series with 313 runs at an average of 52.16. He also took his only Test wicket with his part-time bowling when he caught and bowled Mohammad Yousuf.

This form on the subcontinent continued on 18 February 2006 in England's first warm-up game prior to the Test series against India when Bell top-scored with 78 at Mumbai. He could not maintain this form into the Test series where, in 6 innings, he only scored 131 runs at an average of just under 22.

- **Ian Bell in 2006: Sri Lanka and Pakistan**

After returning from India, Bell had an average start to the season with Warwickshire. He was named in the squad of 13 for the first home Test of the summer, against Sri Lanka, but with the return of Marcus Trescothick, coupled with the good form of Paul Collingwood and the emergence of Alastair Cook, Bell was dropped from the starting 11. Bell was selected in the squad for the 5 match ODI series against Sri Lanka, and was one of only a couple of players to come through the series with any credit.

As a result of this, and the injury to Andrew Flintoff, Bell was recalled to the Test team for the first Test against Pakistan. After spending most of his career batting in the top four, he was asked to bat at number six. He scored a century in each of the first three Tests, becoming the first Englishman since Graham Gooch to score a century in three successive Test matches, but missed his chance to make it four in a row after scoring only 9 in the first innings and being 9 not out when the fourth Test unexpectedly finished a day early after the Pakistan ball tampering row. He finished the series with an average of 93.75, but surprisingly was not awarded the man-of-the-series award for England, with the honour going to Andrew Strauss who averaged 63.42. This run of form (100*, 28, 106*, 119, 4, 9, 9*) gave him an overall Test average of almost 48. Given his average against Australia was only 17, his average against all other sides was around 68. He also played in the ODI series against Pakistan, achieving his two highest scores at the time: 88 at Sophia Gardens and 86* at Trent Bridge, the latter earning him the man-of-the-match award following England's victory.

- **Ian Bell in 2006: Champions Trophy**

In September 2006 Bell was named in the squad for the Champions Trophy in India and also in the squad to tour Australia to attempt to retain the Ashes. In the absence of Marcus Trescothick he was promoted to open the batting for the one-day side. In England's three matches he scored 97 runs, at an average of 32.33. England lost their first two games (to India and Australia) and crashed out of the tournament despite a final group-stage win over eventual runners-up, West Indies.

- **Ian Bell in English cricket team in Australia in 2006-07**

Coming into the Ashes series, with Andrew Flintoff named as captain for the tour and reclaiming his place at number six in the batting order, Bell was viewed as competing with Alastair Cook and Paul Collingwood for two places in the starting eleven. However, because Marcus Trescothick returned to England prior to the first Test, Bell, Cook and Collingwood played in the team throughout the series. Scoring a total of 331 runs, including four half centuries, Bell averaged 33.10 for the series. He failed to convert good starts into big scores, and England suffered a 0 – 5 Test series whitewash. This poor run of results continued into the one-day series: England lost the Twenty20 game and the first of the ODI's. However, England squeaked through into the final of the Commonwealth Bank Series, and dispatched Australia in the finals in two straight games, with Bell scoring 65 in the first of them.

- **Ian Bell in 2007 Cricket World Cup**

Bell was selected as part of England's 15-man squad for the world cup in the West Indies. England had a largely disappointing tournament and Bell's performances were typical of the team as a whole. At the start of the tournament he was selected to bat at number three, as England lost to New Zealand and stuttered to wins over Kenya, Canada and Ireland. Bell suffered an average run of form in these matches, scoring 5, 28, 16 and 31. After defeat to eventual runners up, Sri Lanka, a game in which Bell scored 47, England dropped Ed Joyce from the top of the order and Bell was promoted to open with captain Michael Vaughan. The change in position initially worked well as Bell scored 77 as England lost to Australia, but in the next two games, against Bangladesh and South Africa, he only managed scores of 0 and 7, and was dropped for England's final match against the West Indies, a game which England won. England finished fifth in the Super 8 stage of the tournament and failed to qualify for the semi-finals.

- **Ian Bell in 2007: West Indies and India**

Ian Bell scored the fourth of England's hundreds against the West Indies in the first Test at Lord's in May. Along with Alastair Cook, Paul Collingwood and Matt Prior, they became the first four batsmen for England since 1938 to each score a century in the same Test match. Bell's innings came at number 6 in the batting order and after England declared he had the impressive record at that position of 484 runs at 121.00.

On 21 August 2007, Bell scored his maiden ODI century in the first of seven one-day matches against India, scoring 126 runs off 118 balls (a strike rate of 106.8). Bell went on to score two more fifties in the next two games, including a player-of-the-match 79 at Edgbaston as England took a 2–1 lead in the series. Bell eventually averaged 70.33 for the seven games as England claimed the series 4–3, with a convincing 7 wicket win in the deciding match at Lord's, and Bell was named Man of the Series.

- **Ian Bell in 2007/08: Sri Lanka**

Travelling with the team to Sri Lanka in late September 2007, Bell at first continued his impressive one-day form, scoring 131 from only 121 deliveries, in England's only warm-up match against a Sri Lanka Cricket Board XI. However, Bell struggled with the bat in the subsequent 5-game ODI series, scoring just 70 runs at an average of 14.00.Bell recovered form in the first Test match, scoring 83 and 74, in vain, as England fell to an 88-run defeat. Sri Lanka won the Test series 1–0, after the second and third matches were drawn, and Bell finished the series with a batting average of 43.50.

- **Ian Bell in 2007/08: New Zealand**

Bell initially struggled for form as England opened its five-game ODI series against New Zealand with two heavy defeats, scoring just 5 and 0. However, under pressure for his place in the side, Bell top-scored in England's win in Auckland in the third game of the series with 73 runs, and then made 43 runs from 41 balls as England tied the fourth match, in Napier. Bell managed 24 runs in the final game as New Zealand clinched the series 3–1.

In the first Test match at Hamilton, Bell was hit hard on the wrist during New Zealand's first innings, whilst fielding at short leg. Despite initial fears that his wrist was broken and his tour would be over, the blow turned out to have only caused swelling and bruising. Bell went on to score 25 in England's first innings and top scored in the second innings with an unbeaten 54 as England crumbled to 110 all out and lost the match by 189 runs, the next highest score in the innings being 13 by Alastair Cook. In the second Test, Bell scored 11 and 41 as England won the match to level the series. His finest innings of the tour was in the final Test. After scoring 9 in the first innings, Bell was under some pressure to post a big score. He joined Andrew Strauss at the crease with England 140/3 and the pair proceeded to put on 187 runs and effectively put the match beyond New Zealand. In the process, Bell scored his seventh Test century, and his first overseas for more than two years. He finished the series with a batting average of 50.00, and became the second youngest England player to reach 2,500 runs.

Bell struggled in the home Test series, however, scoring only 45 runs in four innings, with a high score of 21*. He hit some form in the Twenty20 match that followed, top scoring with his highest score in that format, 60*, as England won by nine wickets. He then adopted the opening position for the following ODI series, however his form was intermittent with scores of 46, 0, 20, and 46.

- **Ian Bell in 2008: South Africa, India and West Indies**

Bell started off this series against South Africa by hitting 199 before being dismissed by Paul Harris, one short of his maiden double century, thus becoming the first Englishman to be dismissed on 199. After the initial good start to the tour though, Bell struggled to find form and aside from a 50 in the first innings of the third Test. he did not manage to progress much past the twenties and thirties.

In the final Test against South Africa he made just 28 runs in the match, being dismissed for 24 in the first innings and just four in the second. In the ODI series, he made good scores in the first two matches, hitting 35 in the first match before an unbeaten 28 in the second. He made 73 in the first match as England won by 126 runs. He was less impressive in the fourth match at Lord's, making just 13.

He made 25 in the first ODI against India, but was out for one in the second as England lost by 54 runs. Bell's highest score of the series came in the third match of the series where he made 46, but England still lost the game by 16 runs on the D/L Method. He struggled in the first Test against India, making scores of 17 and seven as England lost the first Test match by 6 wickets. The second Test finished in a draw, although Bell again failed to make a substantial score, being dismissed for just one in the first innings before finishing the second innings on 24 not out.He suffered similarly in India and the West Indies, and following England's dismissal for 51 in the First Test, in which Bell made just four runs, he was dropped in favour of Owais Shah.

- **Ian Bell in 2009: The Ashes**

Bell reacted well to being dropped and began to consistently score runs in the county championship that led to him being named in the 16-man training party for the tests against Australia and captain of the England Lions for their game against Australia, though he failed in that match, scoring 0 (a golden duck) and 20, and remained on the sidelines for the first two Tests of the series.

Bell was selected to play in the third Test at Edgbaston, his home ground, replacing the injured Kevin Pietersen. On his return to the Test side and batting at number three, he scored 53 in England's only innings in a drawn match. The 4th Test Match at Headingley, in which he was twice dismissed edging Mitchell Johnson for scores of eight and three gave Bell his part of a Test record – for the first time in the history of Test cricket the same middle order, three (Ravi Bopara), four (Bell) and five (Paul Collingwood), all failed to reach double figures in either innings, contributing 16 runs between them.

Nonetheless, Bell made 126 against Nottinghamshire at Trent Bridge the next week. He was then selected to play in the final Test at The Oval, and scored 72 to lay a foundation for England's 172-run first-innings lead. Though he was dismissed for four in the second innings, a debut century from Warwickshire colleague Jonathan Trott led England to a 197-run victory, and thus a 2–1 series victory in the Ashes. Bell was dismissed by Mitchell Johnson four times in his five innings in the series, and had scored 140 runs at an average of only 28, though with two half centuries.

On the tour of Bangladesh, Bell scored a quick and confident 84 off 105 balls in England's first innings of the first Test at Chittagong, and scored 39 not out in the second innings. By batting lower down the order, typically at 6, Bell has seen his scores improve and he has scored five of his ten Test centuries whilst batting at 6. In the second test at Mirpur, with England struggling for momentum on 107–3, Bell came to the crease at number 5 making crucial partnerships with Jonathan Trott (67 run partnership), Matt Prior (98 run partnership) and a 143-run stand with Tim Bresnan for the 6th wicket on his way towards his 10th Test match century, finally being dismissed for 138. During his century, Bell's average against Bangladesh touched 488, the highest any batsman has had against a particular country in the history of Test cricket.

- **Ian Bell in 2010: Bangladesh and injury absence**

Bell featured in the home Test series with Bangladesh at the start of the season, scoring a century in the second Test. However, a broken metatarsal sustained in the subsequent one-day series ruled him out of the summer's main series against Pakistan. He did return to action for his county Warwickshire towards the end of the season, scoring a match-winning century as acting captain in the CB40 final against Somerset.

- **Ian Bell fielding during a Test against Sri Lanka in 2011**

By the time the Ashes came around, Bell had a regular place at No. 6 in the team. Throughout the series there were talks of a possible leap up the order, in front of an out-of-form Paul Collingwood. He started off the series well, and progressed throughout the series with many elegant drives, cuts and pulls. However it was not until the 5th Test in Sydney that he could score his first Ashes century after eleven 50s. Bell was one of England's finest with the bat, and helped to contribute to a 3–1 series victory, England's first in Australia since Mike Gatting's men in 1986/87.

- **Ian Bell in 2011: Cricket World Cup**

In the February and March Bangladesh, India, and Sri Lanka hosted the 2011 World Cup. In England's first match they successfully chased a high total by Netherlands, with Bell contributing 33 runs. Next England played India, put up a challenging total of 338. Bell and his captain Strauss set about consolidating England's position, while Bell survived a lbw decision off the bowling of left-arm spinner Yuvraj Singh. Opposition captain Mahendra Singh Dhoni asked for a review. TV replays and Hawk-Eye showed that Bell was indeed plumb. However, since there was a rule wherein the on-field umpire (Billy Bowden here) can have the final decision if the batsman was 2.5 metres forward from the stumps, the umpire stood by his 'not out' decision. Bell went on to make 69 runs and almost helped England win comfortably. This match eventually ended in a tie.

- **Ian Bell in 2011: India**

During the 2011 summer, Bell was an integral part of the team that inflicted a 4 – 0 Test whitewash over the Indian cricket team in friendly home conditions and seaming pitches, helping England to become the number 1 team in the world for the first time since the ICC ranking came into existence. Bell was involved in a controversial run out during the series. Believing the ball to be dead after reaching the boundary, Bell left the middle to head in for tea, however the ball had not actually crossed the boundary and was promptly thrown in by the fielder and the bails taken off. Initially given out, the Indians retracted their appeal at tea and Bell returned to carry on his innings straight after. Bell scored his first double ton in the series, a test best of 235. For taking this decision the Indian captain, Mahendra Singh Dhoni, won the 'Spirit of the cricket' award at the 2011 ICC Awards.

His innings of 159 against India at Nottingham was nominated to be one of the best Test batting performance of the year 2011 by ESPNCricinfo. For his performances in 2011, he was named in the World Test XI by Cricinfo.

- **Ian Bell in 2012: Pakistan, Sri Lanka and West Indies**

In February, the English Team was whitewashed by Pakistan in the UAE, Bell scored just 51 runs in six innings as the English batsmen were exposed off their Spin technique, particularly picking Saeed Ajmal's doosra. In the first game in Dubai, Bell was dismissed for a duck in the first innings, followed by making just four in the second. In the first innings of the second Test he scored 29, his highest score in the series, but was unable to make an impact in the second innings as England were bowled out for 72 to go 2–0 down in the series. England lost the final game of the series by 71 runs, with. Bell again failing to make an impact.

Bell made 52 in the first innings against Sri Lanka but England went on to lose the game by 75 runs, their fourth straight Test defeat. This meant that England had to win the next game to keep hold of their Number One Test ranking. They went on to do so, winning the match by an innings. Bell made 18 in the first innings and was not required to bat again.

In the first Test against the West Indies. Bell returned to form in his favoured English conditions, hitting scores of 61 and 63 not out. In the third and final test of the series, Bell made 73 not out to help secure a draw for England which meant that they won the series. Bell was named in the 14 member squad for the three-match NatWest ODI series against West Indies starting on 16 June at Southampton. Bell would be the opening partner of Cook in the ODI series. He scored his second one-day hundred as England won the first match of the series. His innings was nominated to be one of the best ODI batting performances of the year by ESPNCricinfo. He continued his good form in the next match, hitting 53 as England won by eight wickets.

- **Ian Bell in 2012–13: India**

Ian Bell started off rather ordinarily in this tour, as he struggled against the Indian spinners on slow spinning and dry pitches. In the first tour match at Brabourne Stadium at Mumbai, he scored just 5 against India A before being dismissed by Yuvraj Singh. He followed it up with a 4 & 28* against Mumbai A. He scored 0 & 22, 5 & 28* in the first two tests. In the 4th test at Nagpur, he scored 1 & 116* (from 306 balls). This unbeaten century on the spinning, dry pitch ensured a stale draw on the 4th Test to win the series 2–1. Then in January 2013, he scored 91 (from 89 balls) in the Palam A Ground at Delhi against India A before being dismissed by Mohit Sharma. However, it was in a losing cause as they lost by 53 runs in Duckworth-Lewis method. Two days later, he scored 108 against Delhi cricket team (dismissed by leg spinner Varun Sood), yet again in a losing cause.

- **Ian Bell in 2013–14: Ashes and New Zealand**

Bell made scores of 5 and 32 in the first test in Brisbane, but England lost the match. He made his highest score of the series, 72 in the second Test, which England again lost by a big margin as Australia went 2–0 in the series. The series was lost after just three games when Australia took a 3–0, lead with Bell making scores of 15 and 60. Bell did not make a half century again in the series as England tour began to fall apart after losing the Ashes. He made 27 runs in the fourth Test, which included a duck, before making just 18 runs in the final Test as Australia won the series 5–0.

Senior batsmen such as Bell, Cook and Pietersen were criticised in the English media for their lack of runs, with

Bell himself making just two half centuries and failing to score a hundred in the series. Bell showed good form in the opening two ODIs, making a score of 41 in the first match before being run out for 68 in the second. Despite this, England went on to lose both matches. In the third ODI Bell made 29 before being run out for the second consecutive match. England won their only game of the tour in the fourth ODI, with Bell making 55. He made 14 in the final match as Australia won the series 4–1.

He played in the drawn three test series in New Zealand in March 2013, scoring an obdurate 75 in the last test at Auckland to help England to secure a draw similar to that at Cardiff against Australia in 2009.

- **Ian Bell in 2014: Sri Lanka and India**

Bell was named in the ODI squad for their series against Sri Lanka. He made 50 in the first match of the series as England won by 81 runs on the DL Method. He made 12 in the following match, before hitting an unbeaten 41 in the third match of the series to help England to a ten wicket victory. England lost the final two matches of the series, with Bell making scores of seven and 37 in the next too matches. The two defeats meant that England lost the series 3–2. In the First test, Bell made scores of 56 and 9 as the match ended in a draw. The second and final Test of the series was Bell's 100 Test match. He made 64 in the first innings to help England into a strong position, before making just eight in England's second innings as they collapsed to lose the match.

In the first Test against India Bell made 25 as the match finished in a draw due to a pitch that gave the bowlers little. He was poor in the second Test, making scores of 16 and 1 as

England lost the match to go 1–0 down in the series. Seniors players such as Bell and Alistair Cook came under scrutiny, although retained their places in the squad for the next Test. On 28 July in the third test against India at The Rose Bowl, Southampton, Bell scored a century in the first innings by hitting a six against Ravindra Jadeja when he was at 94 not out. In that over 21 runs of six balls came with Bell scoring 20 with two sixes and two fours. It was Bell's 21st century and first after the previous Ashes series.

He went on to score 167, falling to a ball from Bhuvneshwar Kumar. England eventually went on to win the match by 266 runs and level the series. Bell continued his good form, making 58 in the next match to help England take a 2–1 lead in the series. Bell only made seven in the final match of the series, but due to poor batting from India England clinched the series 3–1. After the first ODI was rained off, Bell opened in the second match of the series, although he made just one as England lost the game. Bell made 28 in the next match as England suffered another defeat. A foot injury suffered in training ruled bell out for the rest of the series.Bell was selected for the tour of Sri Lanka at the back end of 2014. However, he only played in the first two matches, making scores of 35 and 11. England lost both games.

- **Ian Bell in 2015: Tri Series**

Following the removal of Alistair Cook as ODI captain, Bell returned to the top of the order for the tournament against Australia and India. He was out for a duck in the first match against Australia as England lost the opening match. He hit 88 not out in the following match against India to help England win the match. In the following game, he hit 141 against Australia, but it was not enough to prevent another England defeat. In the next game against India he made ten as England qualified for the final. Bell was unable to make an impact in the final, being dismissed for eight as England again lost to Australia.

- **Ian Bell in 2015: West Indies and New Zealand**

Bell was selected in the England squad that toured the West Indies. He made 143 in the first innings of the first Test, but was dismissed for 11 in the second innings after being run out. The match ended in a draw. Bell could only make 1 in England's first innings of the second Test. However, England went on to win the game to take a 1–0 lead in the series. Bell had a poor game in the final match of the series after being dismissed for a duck in both innings. England went on to lose the game by five wickets as the West Indies fought back to level the series at 1–1.

Bell enjoyed a disappointing time in the series against New Zealand. He made just one in the first innings and then followed this up with 29 in the second innings. Despite this, England went on to win the match by 124 runs. Bell's poor form continued in the next Test as he made scores of 12 and one as England lost the game to draw the series 1–1. Bell also dropped several catches in the second Test.

- **Ian Bell in 2020: Retirement**

On September 6, 2020, Bell announced his retirement from all forms of cricket at the end of 2020 Northern summer. This leaves James Anderson as the final active member of 2005 Ashes series team.

- **Ian Bell Personal life**

Bell married wife Chantal in 2011. They honeymooned in the Maldives. She was described by David Lloyd as "A star of a missus." He is a football fan and an Aston Villa supporter and can be seen regularly at Villa Park during games.

TWO

ENGLAND CRICKET TEAM

- **England cricket team**

The England cricket team represents England and Wales in international cricket. Since 1997, it has been governed by the England and Wales Cricket Board (ECB), having been previously governed by Marylebone Cricket Club (the MCC) since 1903. England, as a founding nation, is a Full Member of the International Cricket Council (ICC) with Test, One Day International (ODI) and Twenty20 International (T20I) status. Until the 1990s, Scottish and Irish players also played for England as those countries were not yet ICC members in their own right.

England and Australia were the first teams to play a Test match (15–19 March 1877), and along with South Africa, these nations formed the Imperial Cricket Conference (the predecessor to today's International Cricket Council) on 15 June 1909. England and Australia also played the first ODI on 5 January 1971. England's first T20I was played on 13 June

2005, once more against Australia.

As of 20 December 2022, England have played 1,058 Test matches, winning 387 and losing 317 (with 354 draws). In Test series against Australia, England play for The Ashes, one of the most famous trophies in all of sport, and they have won the urn on 32 occasions. England have also played 773 ODIs, winning 389. They have appeared in the final of the Cricket World Cup four times, winning once in 2019; they have also finished as runners-up in two ICC Champions Trophies (2004 and 2013). England have played 170 T20Is, winning 90. They won the ICC T20 World Cup in 2010 and 2022, and were runners-up in 2016.As of 20 December 2022, England are ranked third in Tests, second in ODIs and second in T20Is by the ICC.

- **The All-England Eleven in 1846**

The first recorded incidence of a team with a claim to represent England comes from 9 July 1739 when an "All-England" team, which consisted of 11 gentlemen from any part of England exclusive of Kent, played against "the Unconquerable County" of Kent and lost by a margin of "very few notches". Such matches were repeated on numerous occasions for the best part of a century.In 1846 William Clarke formed the All-England Eleven. This team eventually competed against a United All-England Eleven with annual matches occurring between 1847 and 1856. These matches were arguably the most important contest of the English season if judged by the quality of the players.

- **The 1859 English team to North America.**

The first overseas tour occurred in September 1859 with England touring North America. This team had six players from the All-England Eleven, six from the United All-England Eleven and was captained by George Parr.With the outbreak of the American Civil War, attention turned elsewhere. English tourists visited Australia in 1861–62 with this first tour organised as a commercial venture by Messrs Spiers and Pond, restaurateurs of Melbourne. Most matches played during tours prior to 1877 were "against odds", with the opposing team fielding more than 11 players to make for a more even contest. This first Australian tour were mostly against odds of at least 18/11.

- **The first England team to tour southern Australia in 1861–62**

The tour was so successful that Parr led a second tour in 1863–64. James Lillywhite led a subsequent England team which sailed on the P&O steamship Poonah on 21 September 1876. They played a combined Australian XI, for once on even terms of 11-a-side. The match, starting on 15 March 1877 at the Melbourne Cricket Ground came to be regarded as the inaugural Test match. The combined Australian XI won this Test match by 45 runs with Charles Bannerman of Australia scoring the first Test century. At the time, the match was promoted as James Lillywhite's XI v Combined Victoria and New South Wales. The teams played a return match on the same ground at Easter, 1877, when Lillywhite's team avenged their loss with a victory by four wickets. The first Test match on English soil occurred in 1880 with England victorious; this was the first time England fielded a fully representative side with W. G. Grace included in the team.

- **1880s**

As a result of this loss, the tour of 1882–83 was dubbed by England captain Ivo Bligh as "the quest to regain the ashes". England, with a mixture of amateurs and professionals, won the series 2–1. Bligh was presented with an urn that contained some ashes, which have variously been said to be of a bail, ball or even a woman's veil, and so The Ashes was born. A fourth match was then played which Australia won by four wickets. However, the match was not considered part of the Ashes series. England dominated many of these early contests, with England winning the Ashes series 10 times between 1884 and 1898. During this period England also played their first Test match against South Africa in 1889 at Port Elizabeth.

- **1890s**

England won the 1890 Ashes series 2–0, with the third match of the series being the first Test match to be abandoned. England lost 2–1 in the 1891–92 series, although England regained the urn the following year. England again won the 1894–95 series, winning 3–2 under the leadership of Andrew Stoddart. In 1895–96, England played South Africa, winning all Tests in the series. The 1899 Ashes series was the first tour where the MCC and the counties appointed a selection committee. There were three active players: Grace, Lord Hawke and Warwickshire captain Herbert Bainbridge. Prior to this, England teams for home Tests had been chosen by the club on whose ground the match was to be played. England lost the 1899 Ashes series 1–0, with Grace making his final Test appearance in the first match of the series.

- **1900s**

The start of the 20th century saw mixed results for England as they lost four of the eight Ashes series between 1900 and 1914. During this period, England lost their first series against South Africa in the 1905–06 season 4–1 as their batting faltered.England lost their first series of the new century to Australia in 1901–02 Ashes. Australia also won the 1902 series, which was memorable for exciting cricket, including Gilbert Jessop scoring a Test century in just 70 minutes. England regained the Ashes in 1904 under the captaincy of Pelham Warner. R. E. Foster scored 287 on his debut and Wilfred Rhodes took 15 wickets in a match. In 1905–06, England lost 4–1 against South Africa. England avenged the defeat in 1907, when they won the series 1–0 under the captaincy of Foster. However, they lost the 1909 Ashes series against Australia, suing 25 players in the process. England also lost to South Africa, with Jack Hobbs scoring his first of 15 centuries on the tour.

- **1910s**

England toured Australia in 1911–12 and beat their opponents 4–1. The team included the likes of Rhodes, Hobbs, Frank Woolley and Sydney Barnes. England lost the first match of the series but bounced back and won the next four Tests. This proved to be the last Ashes series before the war.The 1912 season saw England take part in a unique experiment. A nine-Test triangular tournament involving England, South Africa and Australia was set up. The series was hampered by a very wet summer and player disputes however and the tournament was considered a failure with the Daily Telegraph stating.Nine Tests provide a surfeit of cricket, and contests between Australia and South Africa are not a great attraction to the British public.

With Australia sending a weakened team and the South African bowlers being ineffective England dominated the tournament winning four of their six matches. The match between Australia and South Africa at Lord's was visited by King George V, the first time a reigning monarch had watched Test cricket. England went on one more tour before the outbreak of the First World War, beating South Africa 4–0, with Barnes taking 49 wickets in the series.

- **1920s**

English cricket team at the Test match at the Brisbane Exhibition Ground in 1928. England won by a record margin of 675 runs.England's first match after the war was in the 1920–21 season against Australia. Still feeling the effects of the war England went down to a series of crushing defeats and suffered their first whitewash losing the series 5–0. Six Australians scored hundreds while Mailey spun out 36 English batsmen. Things were no better in the next few Ashes series losing the 1921 Ashes series 3–0 and the 1924–25 Ashes 4–1. England's fortunes were to change in 1926 as they regained the Ashes and were a formidable team during this period dispatching Australia 4–1 in the 1928–29 Ashes tour.

On the same year the West Indies became the fourth nation to be granted Test status and played their first game against England. England won each of these three Tests by an innings, and a view was expressed in the press that their elevation had proved a mistake although Learie Constantine did the double on the tour. In the 1929–30 season England went on two concurrent tours with one team going to New Zealand (who were granted Test status earlier that year) and the other to the West Indies. Despite sending two separate teams England won both tours beating New Zealand 1–0 and the West Indies 2–1.

- **1930s**

Bill Woodfull evades a Bodyline ball. Note the number of leg-side fielders.The 1930 Ashes series saw a young Don Bradman dominate the tour, scoring 974 runs in his seven Test innings. He scored 254 at Lord's, 334 at Headingley and 232 at The Oval. Australia regained the Ashes winning the series 3–1. As a result of Bradman's prolific run-scoring the England captain Douglas Jardine chose to develop the already existing leg theory into fast leg theory, or bodyline, as a tactic to stop Bradman. Fast leg theory involved bowling fast balls directly at the batsman's body. The batsman would need to defend himself, and if he touched the ball with the bat, he risked being caught by one of a large number of fielders placed on the leg side.

Using Jardine's fast leg theory, England won the next Ashes series 4–1, but complaints about the Bodyline tactic caused crowd disruption on the tour, and threats of diplomatic action from the Australian Cricket Board, which during the tour sent the following cable to the MCC in London:

Bodyline bowling assumed such proportions as to menace best interests of game, making protection of body by batsmen the main consideration. Causing intensely bitter feeling between players as well as injury. In our opinion is unsportsmanlike. Unless stopped at once likely to upset friendly relations existing between Australia and England.Later, Jardine was removed from the captaincy and the Laws of Cricket changed so that no more than one fast ball aimed at the body was permitted per over, and having more than two fielders behind square leg was banned.

England's following tour of India in the 1933–34 season was the first Test match to be staged in the subcontinent. The series was also notable for Stan Nichols and Nobby Clark bowling so many bouncers that the Indian batsman wore solar toupées instead of caps to protect themselves.Australia won the 1934 Ashes series 2–1 and kept the urn for the following 19 years. Many of the wickets of the time were friendly to batsmen resulting in a large proportion of matches ending in high scoring draws and many batting records being set.

England drew the 1938 Ashes, meaning Australia retained the urn. England went into the final match of the series at The Oval 1–0 down, but won the final game by an innings and 579 runs. Len Hutton made the highest ever Test score by an Englishman, making 364 in England first innings to help them reach 903, their highest ever score against Australia.

The 1938–39 tour of South Africa saw another experiment with the deciding Test being a timeless Test that was played to a finish. England lead 1–0 going into the final timeless match at Durban. Despite the final Test being 'timeless', the game ended in a draw after 10 days as England had to catch the train to catch the boat home. A record 1,981 runs were scored, and the concept of timeless Tests was abandoned. England went on one final tour of the West Indies in 1939 before the Second World War, although a team for an MCC tour of India was selected more in hope than expectation of the matches being played.

- **1940s**

Test cricket resumed after the war in 1946, and England won their first match back against India. However, they struggled in the 1946–47 Ashes series, losing 3–0 in Australia under Wally Hammond's captaincy. England beat South Africa 3–0 in 1947 with Denis Compton scoring 1,187 runs in the series.

The 1947–48 series against the West Indies was another disappointment for England, with the side losing 2–0 following injuries to several key players. England suffered further humiliation against Bradman's invincible side in the 1948 Ashes series. Hutton was controversially dropped for the third Test, and England were bowled out for just 52 at The Oval. The series proved to be Bradman's final Ashes series.

In 1948–49, England beat South Africa 2–0 under the captaincy of George Mann. The series included a record breaking stand of 359 between Hutton and Cyril Washbrook. The decade ended with England drawing the Test series against New Zealand, with every match ending in a draw.

- **1950s**

Their fortunes changed on the 1953 Ashes tour as they won the series 1–0. England did not lose a series between their 1950–51 and 1958–59 tours of Australia and secured famous victory in 1954–55 under the captaincy of Len Hutton, thanks to Frank Tyson whose 6/85 at Sydney and 7/27 at Melbourne are remembered as the fastest bowling ever seen in Australia. The 1956 series was remembered for the bowling of Jim Laker who took 46 wickets at an average of 9.62, including figures of 19/90 at Old Trafford. After drawing to South Africa, England defeated the West Indies and New Zealand comfortably.

The England team then left for Australia in the 1958–59 season with a team that had been hailed as the strongest ever to leave on an Ashes tour but lost the series 4–0 as Richie Benaud's revitalised Australians were too strong, with England struggling with the bat throughout the series.On 24 August 1959, England inflicted its only 5–0 whitewash over India. All out for 194 at The Oval, India lost the last test by an innings. England's batsman Ken Barrington and Colin Cowdrey both had an excellent series with the bat, with Barrington scoring 357 runs across the series and Cowdrey scoring 344.

- **1960s**

The early and middle 1960s were poor periods for English cricket. Despite England's strength on paper, Australia held the Ashes and the West Indies dominated England in the early part of the decade. May stood down as captain in 1961 following the 1961 Ashes defeat.

Ted Dexter succeeded him as captain but England continued to suffer indifferent results. In 1961–62, they beat Pakistan, but also lost to India. The following year saw England and Australia tie the 1962–63 Ashes series 1–1, meaning Australia retained the urn. Despite beating New Zealand 3–0, England went on to lose to the West Indies, and again failed in the 1964 Ashes, losing the home series 1–0, which marked the end of Dexter's captaincy.

However, from 1968 to 1971 they played 27 consecutive Test matches without defeat, winning 9 and drawing 18 (including the abandoned Test at Melbourne in 1970–71). The sequence began when they drew with Australia at Lord's in the Second Test of the 1968 Ashes series and ended in 1971 when India won the Third Test at The Oval by four wickets. They played 13 Tests with only one defeat immediately beforehand and so played a total of 40 consecutive Tests with only one defeat, dating from their innings victory over the West Indies at The Oval in 1966. During this period they beat New Zealand, India, the West Indies, and Pakistan, and under Ray Illingworth's leadership, regained The Ashes from Australia in 1970–71.

- **1970s**

The 1970s, for the England team, can be largely split into three parts. Early in the decade, Illingworth's side dominated world cricket, winning the Ashes away in 1971 and then retaining them at home in 1972. The same side beat Pakistan at home in 1971 and played by far the better cricket against India that season. However, England were largely helped by the rain to sneak the Pakistan series 1–0 but the same rain saved India twice and one England collapse saw them lose to India. This was, however, one of (if not the) strongest England team ever with the likes of Illingworth, Geoffrey Boycott, John Edrich, Basil D'Oliveira, Dennis Amiss, Alan Knott, John Snow and Derek Underwood at its core.

The mid-1970s were more turbulent. Illingworth and several others had refused to tour India in 1972–73 which led to a clamour for Illingworth's job by the end of that summer – England had just been beaten 2–0 by a flamboyant West Indies side – with several England players well over 35. Mike Denness was the surprising choice but only lasted 18 months; his results against poor opposition were good, but England were badly exposed as ageing and lacking in good fast bowling against the 1974–75

Australians, losing that series 4–1 to lose the Ashes.Denness was replaced in 1975 by Tony Greig. While he managed to avoid losing to Australia, his side were largely thrashed the following year by the young and very much upcoming West Indies for whom Greig's infamous "grovel" remark acted as motivation. Greig's finest hour was probably the 1976–77 win over India in India. When Greig was discovered as being instrumental in World Series Cricket, he was sacked, and replaced by Mike Brearley.

Brearley's side showed again the hyperbole that is often spoken when one side dominates in cricket. While his side of 1977–80 contained some young players who went on to become England greats, most notably future captains Ian Botham, David Gower and Graham Gooch, their opponents were often very much weakened by the absence of their World Series players, especially in 1978, when England beat New Zealand 3–0 and Pakistan 2–0 before thrashing what was effectively Australia's 2nd XI 5–1 in 1978–79.

- **1980s**

The England team, with Brearley's exit in 1980, was never truly settled throughout the 1980s, which will probably be remembered as a low point for the team. While some of the great players like Botham, Gooch and Gower had fine careers, the team seldom succeeded in beating good opposition throughout the decade and did not score a home Test victory (except against minnows Sri Lanka) between September 1985 and July 1990.

Botham took over the captaincy in 1980 and they put up a good fight against the West Indies, losing a five match Test series 1–0, although England were humbled in the return series. After scoring a pair in the first Test against Australia,

Botham lost the captaincy due to his poor form, and was replaced by Brearley. Botham returned to form and played exceptionally in the remainder of the series, being named man of the match in the third, fourth and fifth Tests. The series became known as Botham's Ashes as England recorded a 3–1 victory.

Keith Fletcher took over as captain in 1981, but England lost his first series in charge against India. Bob Willis took over as captain in 1982 and enjoyed victories over India and Pakistan, but lost the Ashes after Australia clinched the series 2–1. England hosted the World Cup in 1983 and reached the semi-finals, but their Test form remained poor, as they suffered defeats against New Zealand, Pakistan and the West Indies.Gower took over as skipper in 1984 and led the team to a 2–1 victory over India. They went on to win the 1985 Ashes 3–1, although after this came a poor run of form. Defeat to the West Indies dented the team's confidence, and they went on to lose to India 2–0. In 1986, Micky Stewart was appointed the first full-time England coach. England beat New Zealand, but there was little hope of them retaining the Ashes in 1986–87. However, despite being described as a team that 'can't bat, can't bowl and can't field', they went on to win the series 2–1.

After losing consecutive series against Pakistan, England drew a three match Test series against New Zealand 0–0. They reached the final of the 1987 World Cup, but lost by seven runs against Australia. After losing 4–0 to the West Indies, England lost the Ashes to a resurgent Australia led by Allan Border. With the likes of Gooch banned following a rebel tour to South Africa, a new look England side suffered defeat again against the West Indies, although this time by a margin of 2–1.

- **1990s**

If the 1980s were a low point for English Test cricket, then the 1990s were only a slight improvement. The arrival of Gooch as captain in 1990 forced a move toward more professionalism and especially fitness though it took some time for old habits to die. Even in 2011, one or two successful county players have been shown up as physically unfit for international cricket. Creditable performances against India and New Zealand in 1990 were followed by a hard-fought draw against the 1991 West Indies and a strong performance in the 1992 Cricket World Cup in which the England team finished as runners-up for the second consecutive World Cup, but landmark losses against Australia in 1990–91 and especially Pakistan in 1992 showed England up badly in terms of bowling. So bad was England's bowling in 1993 that Rod Marsh described England's pace attack at one point as "pie throwers". Having lost three of the first four Tests played in England in 1993, Gooch resigned to be replaced by Michael Atherton.

More selectorial problems abounded during Atherton's reign as new chairman of selectors and coach Ray Illingworth (then into his 60s) assumed almost sole responsibility for the team off the field. The youth policy which had seen England emerge from the West Indies tour of 1993–94 with some credit (though losing to a seasoned Windies team) was abandoned and players such as Gatting and Gooch were persisted with when well into their 30s and 40s. England continued to do well at home against weaker opponents such as India, New Zealand and a West Indies side beginning to fade but struggled badly against improving sides like Pakistan and South Africa. Atherton had offered his resignation after losing the 1997 Ashes series 3–2 having been 1–0 up after two matches – eventually to resign one series later in early 1998. England, looking for talent, went through a whole raft of new players during this period, such as Ronnie Irani, Adam Hollioake, Craig White, Graeme Hick and Mark Ramprakash. At this time, there were two main problems:

The lack of a genuine all-rounder to bat at 6, Botham having left a huge gap in the batting order when he retired from Tests in 1992.Alec Stewart, a sound wicket-keeper and an excellent player of quick bowling, could not open and keep wicket, hence his batting down the order, where he was often exposed to spin which he did not play as well.

Stewart took the reins as captain in 1998, but another losing Ashes series and early World Cup exit cost him Test and ODI captaincy in 1999. This should not detract from the 1998 home Test series where England showed great fortitude to beat a powerful South African side 2–1.

Another reason for their poor performances were the demands of County Cricket teams on their players, meaning that England could rarely field a full-strength team on their tours. This eventually led to the ECB taking over from the MCC as the governing body of England and the implementation of central contracts. 1992 also saw Scotland sever ties with the England and Wales team, and begin to compete as the Scotland national team.

By 1999, with coach David Lloyd resigning after the World Cup exit and new captain Nasser Hussain just appointed, England hit rock bottom (literally ranked as the lowest-rated Test nation) after losing 2–1 to New Zealand in shambolic fashion. Hussain was booed on the Oval balcony as the crowd jeered "We've got the worst team in the world" to the tune of "He's Got the Whole World in His Hands".

- **2000s**

Central contracts were installed – reducing players workloads – and following the arrival of Zimbabwean coach Duncan Fletcher, England thrashed the fallen West Indies 3–1. England's results in Asia improved that winter with series wins against both Pakistan and Sri Lanka. Hussain's side had a far harder edge to it, avoiding the anticipated "Greenwash" in the 2001 Ashes series against the all-powerful Australian team. The nucleus the side was slowly coming together as players such as Hussain himself, Graham Thorpe, Darren Gough and Ashley Giles began to be regularly selected. By 2003 though, having endured another Ashes drubbing as well as another first-round exit from the World Cup, Hussain resigned as captain after one Test against South Africa.

Michael Vaughan took over, with players encouraged to express themselves. England won five consecutive Test series prior to facing Australia in the 2005 Ashes series, taking the team to second place in the ICC Test Championship table. During this period England defeated the West Indies home and away, New Zealand, and Bangladesh at home, and South Africa in South Africa. In June 2005, England played its first ever T20 international match, defeating Australia by 100 runs. Later that year, England defeated Australia 2–1 in a thrilling series to regain the Ashes for the first time in 16 years, having lost them in 1989. Following the 2005 Ashes win, the team suffered from a spate of serious injuries to key players such as Vaughan, Giles, Andrew Flintoff and Simon Jones. As a result, the team underwent an enforced period of transition. A 2–0 defeat in Pakistan was followed by two drawn away series with India and Sri Lanka.

In the home Test series victory against Pakistan in July and August 2006, several promising new players emerged. Most notable were the left-arm orthodox spin bowler Monty Panesar, the first Sikh to play Test cricket for England, and left-handed opening batsman Alastair Cook. The 2006–07 Ashes series was keenly anticipated and was expected to provide a level of competition comparable to the 2005 series. In the event, England, captained by Flintoff who was deputising for the injured Vaughan, lost all five Tests to concede the first Ashes whitewash in 86 years.

In the 2007 Cricket World Cup, England lost to most of the Test playing nations they faced, beating only the West Indies and Bangladesh, although they also avoided defeat by any of the non-Test playing nations. Even so, the unimpressive nature of most of their victories in the tournament, combined with heavy defeats by New Zealand, Australia and South Africa, left many commentators criticising the manner in which the England team approached the one-day game. Coach Duncan Fletcher resigned after eight years in the job as a result and was succeeded by former Sussex coach Peter Moores.

In 2007–08, England toured Sri Lanka and New Zealand, losing the first series 1–0 and winning the second 2–1. These series were followed up at home in May 2008 with a 2–0 home series win against New Zealand, with the results easing pressure on Moores – who was not at ease with his team, particularly star batsman Kevin Pietersen. Pietersen succeeded Vaughan as captain in June 2008, after England had been well beaten by South Africa at home. The poor relationship between the two came to a head on the 2008–09 tour to India. England lost the series 1–0 and both men resigned their positions, although Pietersen remained a member of the England team. Moores was replaced as coach by Zimbabwean Andy Flower. Against this background, England toured the West Indies under the captaincy of Andrew Strauss and, in a disappointing performance, lost the Test series 1–0.

The 2009 Ashes series featured the first Test match played in Wales, at Sophia Gardens, Cardiff. England drew the match thanks to a last-wicket stand by bowlers James Anderson and Panesar. A victory for each team followed before the series was decided at The Oval. Thanks to fine bowling by Stuart Broad and Graeme Swann and a debut century by Jonathan Trott, England regained the Ashes.

- **2010s**

2019 World cup winning team with prime minister Theresa May After a drawn Test series in South Africa, England won their first ever ICC world championship, the 2010 World Twenty20, with a seven-wicket win over Australia in Barbados. The following winter in the 2010–11 Ashes, they beat Australia 3–1 to retain the urn and record their first series win in Australia for 24 years. Furthermore, all three of their wins were by an innings – the first time a touring side had ever recorded three innings victories in a single Test series. Cook earned Man of the Series with 766 runs.

England struggled to match their Test form in the 2011 Cricket World Cup. Despite beating South Africa and tying with eventual winners India, England suffered shock losses to Ireland and Bangladesh before losing in the quarter-finals to Sri Lanka. However the team's excellent form in the Test match arena continued and on 13 August 2011, they became the world's top-ranked Test team after comfortably whitewashing India 4–0, their sixth consecutive series victory and eighth in the past nine series. However, this status only lasted a year – having lost 3–0 to Pakistan over the winter, England were beaten 2–0 by South Africa, who replaced them at the top of the rankings. It was their first home series loss since 2008, against the same opposition.

This loss saw the resignation of Strauss as captain (and his retirement from cricket). Cook, who was already in charge of the ODI side, replaced Strauss and led England to a 2–1 victory in India – their first in the country since 1984–85. In doing so, he became the first captain to score centuries in his first five Tests as captain and became England's leading century-maker with 23 centuries to his name.

- **The England team celebrate victory over Australia in the 2015 Ashes series**

After finishing as runners-up in the ICC Champions Trophy, England faced Australia in back-to-back Ashes series. A 3–0 home win secured England the urn for the fourth time in five series. However, in the return series, they found themselves utterly demolished in a 5–0 defeat, their second Ashes whitewash in under a decade. Their misery was compounded by batsman Jonathan Trott leaving the tour early due to a stress-related illness and the mid-series retirement of spinner Graeme Swann. Following the tour, head coach Flower resigned his post while Pietersen was dropped indefinitely from the England team. Flower was replaced by his predecessor, Moores, but he was sacked for a second time after a string of disappointing results including failing to advance from the group stage at the 2015 World Cup. He was replaced by Australian Trevor Bayliss who oversaw an upturn of form in the ODI side, including series victories against New Zealand and Pakistan. In the Test arena, England reclaimed the Ashes 3–2 in the summer of 2015.

England entered the 2019 Cricket World Cup as favourites, having been ranked the number one ODI side by the ICC for over a year prior to the tournament. However, shock defeats to Pakistan and Sri Lanka during the group stage left them on the brink of elimination and needing to win their final two games against India and New Zealand to guarantee progression to the semi-finals. This was achieved, putting their campaign back on track, and an eight-wicket victory over Australia in the semi-final at Edgbaston meant England were in their first World Cup final since 1992. The final against New Zealand at Lord's has been described as one of the greatest and most dramatic matches in the history of cricket, with some calling it the "greatest ODI in history", as both the match and subsequent Super Over were tied, after England went into the final over of their innings 14 runs behind New Zealand's total. England won by virtue of having scored more boundaries throughout the match, securing their maiden World Cup title in their fourth final appearance.

- **England and Wales Cricket Board**

The England and Wales Cricket Board (ECB) is the governing body of English cricket and the England cricket team. The Board has been operating since 1 January 1997 and represents England on the International Cricket Council. The ECB is also responsible for the generation of income from the sale of tickets, sponsorship and broadcasting rights, primarily in relation to the England team. The ECB's income in the 2006 calendar year was £77 million.

Prior to 1997, the Test and County Cricket Board (TCCB) was the governing body for the English team. Apart from in Test matches, when touring abroad, the England team officially played as MCC up to and including the 1976–77 tour of Australia, reflecting the time when MCC had been responsible for selecting the touring party. The last time the England touring team wore the bacon-and-egg colours of the MCC was on the 1996–97 tour of New Zealand.

- **Status of Wales**

Historically, the England team represented the whole of Great Britain in international cricket, with Scottish or Welsh national teams playing sporadically and players from both countries occasionally representing England. Scotland became an independent member of the ICC in 1994, having severed links with the TCCB two years earlier.

Criticism has been made of the England and Wales Cricket Board using only the England name while utilising Welsh players such as Simon and Geraint Jones. With Welsh players pursuing international careers exclusively with an England team, there have been a number of calls for Wales to become an independent member of the ICC, or for the ECB to provide more fixtures for a Welsh national team. However, both Cricket Wales and Glamorgan County Cricket Club have continually supported the ECB, with Glamorgan arguing for the financial benefits of the Welsh county within the English structure, and Cricket Wales stating they are "committed to continuing to play a major role within the ECB"

The absence of a Welsh cricket team has seen a number of debates within the Welsh Senedd. In 2013 a debate saw both Conservative and Labour members lend their support to the establishment of an independent Welsh team.

In 2015, a report produced by the Welsh National Assembly's petitions committee, reflected the passionate debate around the issue. Bethan Jenkins, Plaid Cymru's spokesperson on heritage, culture, sport and broadcasting, and a member of the petitions committee, argued that Wales should have its own international team and withdraw from the ECB. Jenkins noted that Ireland (with a population of 6.4 million) was an ICC member with 6,000 club players whereas Wales (with 3 million) had 7,500. Jenkins said: "Cricket Wales and Glamorgan CCC say the idea of a Welsh national cricket team is 'an emotive subject', of course having a national team is emotive, you only have to look at the stands during any national game to see that. To suggest this as anything other than natural is a bit of a misleading argument."

In 2017, the First Minister of Wales, Carwyn Jones called for the reintroduction of the Welsh one-day team stating: " is odd that we see Ireland and Scotland playing in international tournaments and not Wales."

- **Team colours**

1. 1994–1996Tetley Bitter
2. 1996–1998ASICS
3. 1998–2000Vodafone
4. 2000–2008Admiral
5. 2008–2010Adidas
6. 2010–2014Brit Insurance
7. 2014–2017Waitrose
8. 2017–2021New BalanceNatWest
9. 2021–2022Cinch

10. 2022–presentCastore

In February 2021, England and Wales Cricket Board announced that England's Principal partner NatWest has been replaced by Cinch, an online used car marketplace. England's kit is manufactured by Castore, who replaced previous manufacturer New Balance in April 2022.

When playing Test cricket, England's cricket whites feature the three lions badge on the left of the shirt and the name of the sponsor Cinch on the centre. English fielders may wear a navy blue cap or white sun hat with the ECB logo in the middle. Helmets are also coloured navy blue. Before 1997 the uniform sported the TCCB lion and stumps logo on the uniforms, while the helmets, jumpers and hats had the three lions emblem.

In limited overs cricket, England's ODI and Twenty20 shirts feature the Cinch logo across the centre, with the three lions badge on the left of the shirt and the New Balance logo on the right. In ODIs, the kit comprises a blue shirt with navy trousers, whilst the Twenty20 kit comprises a flame red shirt and navy trousers. In ICC limited-overs tournaments, a modified kit design is used with sponsor's logo moving to the sleeve and 'ENGLAND' printed across the front.Over the years, England's ODI kit has cycled between various shades of blue (such as a pale blue used until the mid-1990s, when it was replaced in favour of a bright blue)with the occasional all-red kit.In April 2017, ECB brought back traditional cable-knit sweater for test matches under new supplier New Balance.

THREE

Let's Know About Cricket

- **Let's Know About Cricket**

Cricket is a bat-and-ball game played between two teams of eleven players on a field at the centre of which is a 22-yard (20-metre) pitch with a wicket at each end, each comprising two bails balanced on three stumps. The game proceeds when a player on the fielding team, called the bowler, "bowls" (propels) the ball from one end of the pitch towards the wicket at the other end. The batting side's players score runs by striking the bowled ball with a bat and running between the wickets, while the bowling side tries to prevent this by keeping the ball within the field and getting it to either wicket, and dismiss each batter (so they are "out"). Means of dismissal include being bowled, when the ball hits the stumps and dislodges the bails, and by the fielding side either catching a hit ball before it touches the ground, or hitting a wicket with the ball before a batter can cross the crease line in front of the wicket to complete a run. When ten batters have been dismissed, the innings ends and the teams swap roles. The game is adjudicated by two umpires, aided by a third umpire and match referee in international matches.

Forms of cricket range from Twenty20, with each team batting for a single innings of 20 overs and the game generally lasting three hours, to Test matches played over five days. Traditionally cricketers play in all-white kit, but in limited overs cricket they wear club or team colours. In addition to the basic kit, some players wear protective gear to prevent injury caused by the ball, which is a hard, solid spheroid made of compressed leather with a slightly raised sewn seam enclosing a cork core layered with tightly wound string.

The earliest reference to cricket is in South East England in the mid-16th century. It spread globally with the expansion of the British Empire, with the first international matches in the second half of the 19th century. The game's governing body is the International Cricket Council (ICC), which has over 100 members, twelve of which are full members who play Test matches. The game's rules, the Laws of Cricket, are maintained by Marylebone Cricket Club (MCC) in London. The sport is followed primarily in South Asia, Australasia, the United Kingdom, southern Africa and the West Indies.Women's cricket, which is organised and played separately, has also achieved international standard. The most successful side playing international cricket is Australia, which has won seven One Day International trophies, including five World Cups, more than any other country and has been the top-rated Test side more than any other country.

- **History of cricket to 1725**

Cricket is one of many games in the "club ball" sphere that basically involve hitting a ball with a hand-held implement; others include baseball (which shares many similarities with cricket, both belonging in the more specific bat-and-ball games category), golf, hockey, tennis, squash, badminton and table tennis. In cricket's case, a key difference is the existence of a solid target structure, the wicket (originally, it is thought, a "wicket gate" through which sheep were herded), that the batter must defend. The cricket historian Harry Altham identified three "groups" of "club ball" games: the "hockey group", in which the ball is driven to and fro between two targets (the goals); the "golf group", in which the ball is driven towards an undefended target (the hole); and the "cricket group", in which "the ball is aimed at a mark (the wicket) and driven away from it".

It is generally believed that cricket originated as a children's game in the south-eastern counties of England, sometime during the medieval period.Although there are claims for prior dates, the earliest definite reference to cricket being played comes from evidence given at a court case in Guildford in January 1597 (Old Style), equating to January 1598 in the modern calendar. The case concerned ownership of a certain plot of land and the court heard the testimony of a 59-year-old coroner, John Derrick, who gave witness that.

Being a scholler in the ffree schoole of Guldeford hee and diverse of his fellows did runne and play there at creckett and other plaies.

Given Derrick's age, it was about half a century earlier when he was at school and so it is certain that cricket was being played c. 1550 by boys in Surrey. The view that it was originally a children's game is reinforced by Randle Cotgrave's 1611 English-French dictionary in which he defined the noun "crosse" as "the crooked staff wherewith boys play at cricket" and the verb form "crosser" as "to play at cricket".

One possible source for the sport's name is the Old English word "cryce" (or "cricc") meaning a crutch or staff. In Samuel Johnson's Dictionary, he derived cricket from "cryce, Saxon, a stick". In Old French, the word "criquet" seems to have meant a kind of club or stick. Given the strong medieval trade connections between south-east England and the County of Flanders when the latter belonged to the Duchy of Burgundy, the name may have been derived from the Middle Dutch (in use in Flanders at the time) "krick"(-e), meaning a stick (crook). Another possible source is the Middle Dutch word "krickstoel", meaning a long low stool used for kneeling in church and which resembled the long low wicket with two stumps used in early cricket. According to Heiner Gillmeister, a European language expert of Bonn University, "cricket" derives from the Middle Dutch phrase for hockey, met de (krik ket)sen (i.e., "with the stick chase"). Gillmeister has suggested that not only the name but also the sport itself may be of Flemish origin.

- **Growth of amateur and professional cricket in England**

Evolution of the cricket bat. The original "hockey stick" (left) evolved into the straight bat from c. 1760 when pitched delivery bowling began.

Although the main object of the game has always been to score the most runs, the early form of cricket differed from the modern game in certain key technical aspects; the North American variant of cricket known as wicket retained many of these aspects. The ball was bowled underarm by the bowler and along the ground towards a batter armed with a bat that in shape resembled a hockey stick; the batter defended a low, two-stump wicket; and runs were called notches because the scorers recorded them by notching tally sticks.

In 1611, the year Cotgrave's dictionary was published, ecclesiastical court records at Sidlesham in Sussex state that two parishioners, Bartholomew Wyatt and Richard Latter, failed to attend church on Easter Sunday because they were playing cricket. They were fined 12d each and ordered to do penance.This is the earliest mention of adult participation in cricket and it was around the same time that the earliest known organised inter-parish or village match was played – at Chevening, Kent. In 1624, a player called Jasper Vinall died after he was accidentally struck on the head during a match between two parish teams in Sussex.

Cricket remained a low-key local pursuit for much of the 17th century. It is known, through numerous references found in the records of ecclesiastical court cases, to have been proscribed at times by the Puritans before and during the Commonwealth. The problem was nearly always the issue of Sunday play as the Puritans considered cricket to be "profane" if played on the Sabbath, especially if large crowds or gambling were involved.

According to the social historian Derek Birley, there was a "great upsurge of sport after the Restoration" in 1660. Gambling on sport became a problem significant enough for Parliament to pass the 1664 Gambling Act, limiting stakes to £100 which was, in any case, a colossal sum exceeding the annual income of 99% of the population. Along with prizefighting, horse racing and blood sports, cricket was perceived to be a gambling sport.Rich patrons made matches for high stakes, forming teams in which they engaged the first professional players.By the end of the century, cricket had developed into a major sport that was spreading throughout England and was already being taken abroad by English mariners and colonisers – the earliest reference to cricket overseas is dated 1676. A 1697 newspaper report survives of "a great cricket match" played in Sussex "for fifty guineas apiece" – this is the earliest known contest that is generally considered a First Class match.

- The patrons, and other players from the social class known as the "gentry", began to classify themselves as "amateurs" to establish a clear distinction from the professionals, who were invariably members of the working class, even to the point of having separate changing and dining facilities. The gentry, including such high-ranking nobles as the Dukes of Richmond, exerted their honour code of noblesse oblige to claim rights of leadership in any sporting contests they took part in, especially as it was necessary for them to play alongside their "social inferiors" if they were to win their bets. In time, a perception took hold that the typical amateur who played in first-class cricket, until 1962 when amateurism was abolished, was someone with a public school education who had then gone to one of Cambridge or Oxford University – society insisted that such people were "officers and gentlemen" whose destiny was to provide leadership. In a purely financial sense, the cricketing amateur would theoretically claim expenses for playing while his professional counterpart played under contract and was paid a wage or match fee;

in practice, many amateurs claimed more than actual expenditure and the derisive term "shamateur" was coined to describe the practice.

- **The Young Cricketer, 1768**

The game underwent major development in the 18th century to become England's national sport.Its success was underwritten by the twin necessities of patronage and betting. Cricket was prominent in London as early as 1707 and, in the middle years of the century, large crowds flocked to matches on the Artillery Ground in Finsbury. The single wicket form of the sport attracted huge crowds and wagers to match, its popularity peaking in the 1748 season. Bowling underwent an evolution around 1760 when bowlers began to pitch the ball instead of rolling or skimming it towards the batter. This caused a revolution in bat design because, to deal with the bouncing ball, it was necessary to introduce the modern straight bat in place of the old "hockey stick" shape.

The Hambledon Club was founded in the 1760s and, for the next twenty years until the formation of Marylebone Cricket Club (MCC) and the opening of Lord's Old Ground in 1787, Hambledon was both the game's greatest club and its focal point. MCC quickly became the sport's premier club and the custodian of the Laws of Cricket. New Laws introduced in the latter part of the 18th century included the three stump wicket and leg before wicket (lbw).

The 19th century saw underarm bowling superseded by first roundarm and then overarm bowling. Both developments were controversial.Organisation of the game at county level led to the creation of the county clubs, starting with Sussex in 1839. In December 1889, the eight leading county clubs formed the official County Championship, which began in 1890.

The most famous player of the 19th century was W. G. Grace, who started his long and influential career in 1865. It was especially during the career of Grace that the distinction between amateurs and professionals became blurred by the existence of players like him who were nominally amateur but, in terms of their financial gain, de facto professional. Grace himself was said to have been paid more money for playing cricket than any professional.

The last two decades before the First World War have been called the "Golden Age of cricket". It is a nostalgic name prompted by the collective sense of loss resulting from the war, but the period did produce some great players and memorable matches, especially as organised competition at county and Test level developed.

- **Cricket becomes an international sport**

In 1844, the first-ever international match took place between the United States and Canada. In 1859, a team of English players went to North America on the first overseas tour. Meanwhile, the British Empire had been instrumental in spreading the game overseas and by the middle of the 19th century it had become well established in Australia, the Caribbean, India, Pakistan, New Zealand, North America and South Africa.

In 1862, an English team made the first tour of Australia. The first Australian team to travel overseas consisted of Aboriginal stockmen who toured England in 1868. The first One Day International match was played on 5 January 1971 between Australia and England at the Melbourne Cricket Ground.

In 1876–77, an England team took part in what was retrospectively recognised as the first-ever Test match at the Melbourne Cricket Ground against Australia. The rivalry between England and Australia gave birth to The Ashes in 1882, and this has remained Test cricket's most famous contest. Test cricket began to expand in 1888–89 when South Africa played England.

- **World cricket in the 20th century**

The inter-war years were dominated by Australia's Don Bradman, statistically the greatest Test batter of all time. Test cricket continued to expand during the 20th century with the addition of the West Indies (1928), New Zealand (1930) and India (1932) before the Second World War and then Pakistan (1952), Sri Lanka (1982), Zimbabwe (1992), Bangladesh (2000), Ireland and Afghanistan (both 2018) in the post-war period. South Africa was banned from international cricket from 1970 to 1992 as part of the apartheid boycott.

- **The rise of limited overs cricket**

Cricket entered a new era in 1963 when English counties introduced the limited overs variant. As it was sure to produce a result, limited overs cricket was lucrative and the number of matches increased. The first Limited Overs International was played in 1971 and the governing International Cricket Council (ICC), seeing its potential, staged the first limited overs Cricket World Cup in 1975. In the 21st century, a new limited overs form, Twenty20, made an immediate impact. On 22 June 2017, Afghanistan and Ireland became the 11th and 12th ICC full members, enabling them to play Test cricket.

- **A typical cricket field.**

In cricket, the rules of the game are specified in a code called The Laws of Cricket (hereinafter called "the Laws") which has a global remit. There are 42 Laws (always written with a capital "L"). The earliest known version of the code was drafted in 1744 and, since 1788, it has been owned and maintained by its custodian, the Marylebone Cricket Club (MCC) in London.

- **Playing area**

Cricket is a bat-and-ball game played on a cricket field between two teams of eleven players each. The field is usually circular or oval in shape and the edge of the playing area is marked by a boundary, which may be a fence, part of the stands, a rope, a painted line or a combination of these; the boundary must if possible be marked along its entire length.

In the approximate centre of the field is a rectangular pitch (see image, below) on which a wooden target called a wicket is sited at each end; the wickets are placed 22 yards (20 m) apart. The pitch is a flat surface 10 feet (3.0 m) wide, with very short grass that tends to be worn away as the game progresses (cricket can also be played on artificial surfaces, notably matting). Each wicket is made of three wooden stumps topped by two bails.

- **Cricket pitch and creases**

As illustrated above, the pitch is marked at each end with four white painted lines: a bowling crease, a popping crease and two return creases. The three stumps are aligned centrally on the bowling crease, which is eight feet eight inches long. The popping crease is drawn four feet in front of the bowling crease and parallel to it; although it is drawn as a twelve-foot line (six feet either side of the wicket), it is, in fact, unlimited in length. The return creases are drawn at right angles to the popping crease so that they intersect the ends of the bowling crease; each return crease is drawn as an eight-foot line, so that it extends four feet behind the bowling crease, but is also, in fact, unlimited in length.

Before a match begins, the team captains (who are also players) toss a coin to decide which team will bat first and so take the first innings. Innings is the term used for each phase of play in the match.In each innings, one team bats, attempting to score runs, while the other team bowls and fields the ball, attempting to restrict the scoring and dismiss the batters. When the first innings ends, the teams change roles; there can be two to four innings depending upon the type of match. A match with four scheduled innings is played over three to five days; a match with two scheduled innings is usually completed in a single day. During an innings, all eleven members of the fielding team take the field, but usually only two members of the batting team are on the field at any given time. The exception to this is if a batter has any type of illness or injury restricting his or her ability to run, in this case the batter is allowed a runner who can run between the wickets when the batter hits a scoring run or runs,though this does not apply in international cricket. The order of batters is usually announced just before the match, but it can be varied.

The main objective of each team is to score more runs than their opponents but, in some forms of cricket, it is also necessary to dismiss all of the opposition batters in their final innings in order to win the match, which would otherwise be drawn. If the team batting last is all out having scored fewer runs than their opponents, they are said to have "lost by n runs" (where n is the difference between the aggregate number of runs scored by the teams). If the team that bats last scores enough runs to win, it is said to have "won by n wickets", where n is the number of wickets left to fall. For example, a team that passes its opponents' total having lost six wickets (i.e., six of their batters have been dismissed) have won the match "by four wickets".

In a two-innings-a-side match, one team's combined first and second innings total may be less than the other side's first innings total. The team with the greater score is then said to have "won by an innings and n runs", and does not need to bat again: n is the difference between the two teams' aggregate scores. If the team batting last is all out, and both sides have scored the same number of runs, then the match is a tie; this result is quite rare in matches of two innings a side with only 62 happening in first-class matches from the earliest known instance in 1741 until January 2017. In the traditional form of the game, if the time allotted for the match expires before either side can win, then the game is declared a draw.

If the match has only a single innings per side, then a maximum number of overs applies to each innings. Such a match is called a "limited overs" or "one-day" match, and the side scoring more runs wins regardless of the number of wickets lost, so that a draw cannot occur. In some cases, ties are broken by having each team bat for a one-over innings known as a Super Over; subsequent Super Overs may be played if the first Super Over ends in a tie. If this kind of match is temporarily interrupted by bad weather, then a complex mathematical formula, known as the Duckworth–Lewis–Stern method after its developers, is often used to recalculate a new target score. A one-day match can also be declared a "no-result" if fewer than a previously agreed number of overs have been bowled by either team, in circumstances that make normal resumption of play impossible; for example, wet weather.

In all forms of cricket, the umpires can abandon the match if bad light or rain makes it impossible to continue. There have been instances of entire matches, even Test matches scheduled to be played over five days, being lost to bad weather without a ball being bowled: for example, the third Test of the 1970/71 series in Australia.

- **Innings**

The innings (ending with 's' in both singular and plural form) is the term used for each phase of play during a match. Depending on the type of match being played, each team has either one or two innings. Sometimes all eleven members of the batting side take a turn to bat but, for various reasons, an innings can end before they have all done so. The innings terminates if the batting team is "all out", a term defined by the Laws: "at the fall of a wicket or the retirement of a batter, further balls remain to be bowled but no further batter is available to come in". In this situation, one of the batters has not been dismissed and is termed not out; this is because he has no partners left and there must always be two active batters while the innings is in progress.

- **An innings may end early while there are still two not out batters**

the batting team's captain may declare the innings closed even though some of his players have not had a turn to bat: this is a tactical decision by the captain, usually because he believes his team have scored sufficient runs and need time to dismiss the opposition in their innings

the set number of overs (i.e., in a limited overs match) have been bowled

the match has ended prematurely due to bad weather or running out of time

in the final innings of the match, the batting side has reached its target and won the game.

- **Overs**

The Laws state that, throughout an innings, "the ball shall be bowled from each end alternately in overs of 6 balls". The name "over" came about because the umpire calls "Over!" when six balls have been bowled. At this point, another bowler is deployed at the other end, and the fielding side changes ends while the batters do not. A bowler cannot bowl two successive overs, although a bowler can (and usually does) bowl alternate overs, from the same end, for several overs which are termed a "spell". The batters do not change ends at the end of the over, and so the one who was non-striker is now the striker and vice versa. The umpires also change positions so that the one who was at "square leg" now stands behind the wicket at the non-striker's end and vice versa.

- **Clothing and equipment**

English cricketer W. G. Grace "taking guard" in 1883. His pads and bat are very similar to those used today. The gloves have evolved somewhat. Many modern players use more defensive equipment than were available to Grace, most notably helmets and arm guards.

The wicket-keeper (a specialised fielder behind the batter) and the batters wear protective gear because of the hardness of the ball, which can be delivered at speeds of more than 145 kilometres per hour (90 mph) and presents a major health and safety concern. Protective clothing includes pads (designed to protect the knees and shins), batting gloves or wicket-keeper's gloves for the hands, a safety helmet for the head and a box for male players inside the trousers (to protect the crotch area). Some batters wear additional padding inside their shirts and trousers such as thigh pads, arm pads, rib protectors and shoulder pads. The only fielders allowed to wear protective gear are those in positions very close to the batter (i.e., if they are alongside or in front of him), but they cannot wear gloves or external leg guards.

Subject to certain variations, on-field clothing generally includes a collared shirt with short or long sleeves; long trousers; woolen pullover (if needed); cricket cap (for fielding) or a safety helmet; and spiked shoes or boots to increase traction. The kit is traditionally all white and this remains the case in Test and first-class cricket but, in limited overs cricket, team colours are worn instead.

- **Bat and ball**

Two types of cricket ball, both of the same size:

i) A used white ball. White balls are mainly used in limited overs cricket, especially in matches played at night, under floodlights (left).

ii) A used red ball. Red balls are used in Test cricket, first-class cricket and some other forms of cricket (right).

The essence of the sport is that a bowler delivers (i.e., bowls) the ball from his or her end of the pitch towards the batter who, armed with a bat, is "on strike" at the other end (see next sub-section: Basic gameplay).

The bat is made of wood, usually Salix alba (white willow), and has the shape of a blade topped by a cylindrical handle. The blade must not be more than 4.25 inches (10.8 cm) wide and the total length of the bat not more than 38 inches (97 cm). There is no standard for the weight, which is usually between 2 lb 7 oz and 3 lb (1.1 and 1.4 kg).

The ball is a hard leather-seamed spheroid, with a circumference of 9 inches (23 cm). The ball has a "seam": six rows of stitches attaching the leather shell of the ball to the string and cork interior. The seam on a new ball is prominent and helps the bowler propel it in a less predictable manner. During matches, the quality of the ball deteriorates to a point where it is no longer usable; during the course of this deterioration, its behaviour in flight will change and can influence the outcome of the match. Players will, therefore, attempt to modify the ball's behaviour by modifying its physical properties. Polishing the ball and wetting it with sweat or saliva is legal, even when the polishing is deliberately done on one side only to increase the ball's swing through the air, but the acts of rubbing other substances into the ball, scratching the surface or picking at the seam are illegal ball tampering.

- **Player roles**

Basic gameplay: bowler to batter

During normal play, thirteen players and two umpires are on the field. Two of the players are batters and the rest are all eleven members of the fielding team. The other nine players in the batting team are off the field in the pavilion. The image with overlay below shows what is happening when a ball is being bowled and which of the personnel are on or close to the pitch.

- **Return crease**

In the photo, the two batters (3 & 8; wearing yellow) have taken position at each end of the pitch (6). Three members of the fielding team (4, 10 & 11; wearing dark blue) are in shot. One of the two umpires (1; wearing white hat) is stationed behind the wicket (2) at the bowler's (4) end of the pitch. The bowler (4) is bowling the ball (5) from his end of the pitch to the batter at the other end who is called the "striker". The other batter (3) at the bowling end is called the "non-striker". The wicket-keeper (10), who is a specialist, is positioned behind the striker's wicket (9) and behind him stands one of the fielders in a position called "first slip" (11). While the bowler and the first slip are wearing conventional kit only, the two batters and the wicket-keeper are wearing protective gear including safety helmets, padded gloves and leg guards (pads).

While the umpire (1) in shot stands at the bowler's end of the pitch, his colleague stands in the outfield, usually in or near the fielding position called "square leg", so that he is in line with the popping crease (7) at the striker's end of the pitch. The bowling crease (not numbered) is the one on which the wicket is located between the return creases (12). The bowler (4) intends to hit the wicket (9) with the ball (5) or, at least, to prevent the striker (8) from scoring runs. The striker (8) intends, by using his bat, to defend his wicket and, if possible, to hit the ball away from the pitch in order to score runs.

Some players are skilled in both batting and bowling, or as either or these as well as wicket-keeping, so are termed all-rounders. Bowlers are classified according to their style, generally as fast bowlers, seam bowlers or spinners. Batters are classified according to whether they are right-handed or left-handed.

- **Fielding**

Of the eleven fielders, three are in shot in the image above. The other eight are elsewhere on the field, their positions determined on a tactical basis by the captain or the bowler. Fielders often change position between deliveries, again as directed by the captain or bowler.

If a fielder is injured or becomes ill during a match, a substitute is allowed to field instead of him, but the substitute cannot bowl or act as a captain, except in the case of concussion substitutes in international cricket. The substitute leaves the field when the injured player is fit to return. The Laws of Cricket were updated in 2017 to allow substitutes to act as wicket-keepers.

- **Bowling and dismissal**

Glenn McGrath of Australia holds the world record for most wickets in the Cricket World Cup.

Most bowlers are considered specialists in that they are selected for the team because of their skill as a bowler, although some are all-rounders and even specialist batters bowl occasionally. The specialists bowl several times during an innings but may not bowl two overs consecutively. If the captain wants a bowler to "change ends", another bowler must temporarily fill in so that the change is not immediate.

A bowler reaches his delivery stride by means of a "run-up" and an over is deemed to have begun when the bowler starts his run-up for the first delivery of that over, the ball then being "in play".

Fast bowlers, needing momentum, take a lengthy run up while bowlers with a slow delivery take no more than a couple of steps before bowling. The fastest bowlers can deliver the ball at a speed of over 145 kilometres per hour (90 mph) and they sometimes rely on sheer speed to try to defeat the batter, who is forced to react very quickly.

Other fast bowlers rely on a mixture of speed and guile by making the ball seam or swing (i.e. curve) in flight. This type of delivery can deceive a batter into miscuing his shot, for example, so that the ball just touches the edge of the bat and can then be "caught behind" by the wicket-keeper or a slip fielder. At the other end of the bowling scale is the spin bowler who bowls at a relatively slow pace and relies entirely on guile to deceive the batter. A spinner will often "buy his wicket" by "tossing one up" (in a slower, steeper parabolic path) to lure the batter into making a poor shot. The batter has to be very wary of such deliveries as they are often "flighted" or spun so that the ball will not behave quite as he expects and he could be "trapped" into getting himself out. In between the pacemen and the spinners are the medium paced seamers who rely on persistent accuracy to try to contain the rate of scoring and wear down the batter's concentration.

There are nine ways in which a batter can be dismissed: five relatively common and four extremely rare. The common forms of dismissal are bowled, caught, leg before wicket (lbw), run out and stumped. Rare methods are hit wicket,hit the ball twice, obstructing the field and timed out. The Laws state that the fielding team, usually the bowler in practice, must appeal for a dismissal before the umpire can give his decision. If the batter is out, the umpire raises a forefinger and says "Out!"; otherwise, he will shake his head and say "Not out".There is, effectively, a tenth method of dismissal, retired out, which is not an on-field dismissal as such but rather a retrospective one for which no fielder is credited.

- **Batting, runs and extras**

The directions in which a right-handed batter, facing down the page, intends to send the ball when playing various cricketing shots. The diagram for a left-handed batter is a mirror image of this one.

Batters take turns to bat via a batting order which is decided beforehand by the team captain and presented to the umpires, though the order remains flexible when the captain officially nominates the team. Substitute batters are generally not allowed, except in the case of concussion substitutes in international cricket.

In order to begin batting the batter first adopts a batting stance. Standardly, this involves adopting a slight crouch with the feet pointing across the front of the wicket, looking in the direction of the bowler, and holding the bat so it passes over the feet and so its tip can rest on the ground near to the toes of the back foot.

A skilled batter can use a wide array of "shots" or "strokes" in both defensive and attacking mode. The idea is to hit the ball to the best effect with the flat surface of the bat's blade. If the ball touches the side of the bat it is called an "edge". The batter does not have to play a shot and can allow the ball to go through to the wicketkeeper. Equally, he does not have to attempt a run when he hits the ball with his bat. Batters do not always seek to hit the ball as hard as possible, and a good player can score runs just by making a deft stroke with a turn of the wrists or by simply "blocking" the ball but directing it away from fielders so that he has time to take a run. A wide variety of shots are played, the batter's repertoire including strokes named according to the style of swing and the direction aimed: e.g., "cut", "drive", "hook", "pull".

The batter on strike (i.e. the "striker") must prevent the ball hitting the wicket, and try to score runs by hitting the ball with his bat so that he and his partner have time to run from one end of the pitch to the other before the fielding side can return the ball. To register a run, both runners must touch the ground behind the popping crease with either their bats or their bodies (the batters carry their bats as they run). Each completed run increments the score of both the team and the striker.

- **Sachin Tendulkar is the only player to have scored one hundred international centuries**

The decision to attempt a run is ideally made by the batter who has the better view of the ball's progress, and this is communicated by calling: usually "yes", "no" or "wait". More than one run can be scored from a single hit: hits worth one to three runs are common, but the size of the field is such that it is usually difficult to run four or more. To compensate for this, hits that reach the boundary of the field are automatically awarded four runs if the ball touches the ground en route to the boundary or six runs if the ball clears the boundary without touching the ground within the boundary. In these cases the batters do not need to run. Hits for five are unusual and generally rely on the help of "overthrows" by a fielder returning the ball. If an odd number of runs is scored by the striker, the two batters have changed ends, and the one who was non-striker is now the striker. Only the striker can score individual runs, but all runs are added to the team's total.

Additional runs can be gained by the batting team as extras (called "sundries" in Australia) due to errors made by the fielding side. This is achieved in four ways: no-ball, a penalty of one extra conceded by the bowler if he breaks the rules; wide, a penalty of one extra conceded by the bowler if he bowls so that the ball is out of the batter's reach bye, an extra awarded if the batter misses the ball and it goes past the wicket-keeper and gives the batters time to run in the conventional way leg bye, as for a bye except that the ball has hit the batter's body, though not his bat. If the bowler has conceded a no-ball or a wide, his team incurs an additional penalty because that ball (i.e., delivery) has to be bowled again and hence the batting side has the opportunity to score more runs from this extra ball.

- **Specialist roles**

Captain (cricket) and Wicket-keeper

The captain is often the most experienced player in the team, certainly the most tactically astute, and can possess any of the main skillsets as a batter, a bowler or a wicket-keeper. Within the Laws, the captain has certain responsibilities in terms of nominating his players to the umpires before the match and ensuring that his players conduct themselves "within the spirit and traditions of the game as well as within the Laws".

The wicket-keeper (sometimes called simply the "keeper") is a specialist fielder subject to various rules within the Laws about his equipment and demeanour. He is the only member of the fielding side who can effect a stumping and is the only one permitted to wear gloves and external leg guards. Depending on their primary skills, the other ten players in the team tend to be classified as specialist batters or specialist bowlers. Generally, a team will include five or six specialist batters and four or five specialist bowlers, plus the wicket-keeper.

- **Umpires and scorers**

The game on the field is regulated by the two umpires, one of whom stands behind the wicket at the bowler's end, the other in a position called "square leg" which is about 15–20 metres away from the batter on strike and in line with the popping crease on which he is taking guard. The umpires have several responsibilities including adjudication on whether a ball has been correctly bowled (i.e., not a no-ball or a wide); when a run is scored; whether a batter is out (the fielding side must first appeal to the umpire, usually with the phrase "How's that?" or "Owzat?"); when intervals start and end; and the suitability of the pitch, field and weather for playing the game. The umpires are authorised to interrupt or even abandon a match due to circumstances likely to endanger the players, such as a damp pitch or deterioration of the light.

Off the field in televised matches, there is usually a third umpire who can make decisions on certain incidents with the aid of video evidence. The third umpire is mandatory under the playing conditions for Test and Limited Overs

International matches played between two ICC full member countries. These matches also have a match referee whose job is to ensure that play is within the Laws and the spirit of the game.

The match details, including runs and dismissals, are recorded by two official scorers, one representing each team. The scorers are directed by the hand signals of an umpire . For example, the umpire raises a forefinger to signal that the batter is out (has been dismissed); he raises both arms above his head if the batter has hit the ball for six runs. The scorers are required by the Laws to record all runs scored, wickets taken and overs bowled; in practice, they also note significant amounts of additional data relating to the game.

A match's statistics are summarised on a scorecard. Prior to the popularisation of scorecards, most scoring was done by men sitting on vantage points cuttings notches on tally sticks and runs were originally called notches.According to Rowland Bowen, the earliest known scorecard templates were introduced in 1776 by T. Pratt of Sevenoaks and soon came into general use.It is believed that scorecards were printed and sold at Lord's for the first time in 1846.

Thank You

Thank You For Reading This Book And Shared This Book To Friends As Birthday Gift Have A Wonderfull Day.

Printed by Libri Plureos GmbH in Hamburg,
Germany